Withdrawn

MONSTER MÂCHÉ ART

Thanks to the creative team:
Editor: Tim Harris
Design: Perfect Bound Ltd

Hungry Tomato®
A division of Lerner Publishing Group, Inc.
241 First Avenue North
Minneapolis, MN 55401 USA

For reading levels and more information, look up this title at www.lernerbooks.com.

Main body text set in CocogooseNarrow Semi Light.

Library of Congress Cataloging-in-Publication Data

Names: Kington, Emily, 1961–
Title: Monster mâché art / by Emily Kington.
Description: Minneapolis : Hungry Tomato, [2019] | Series: Wild art projects | Includes index. | Audience: Age 8–12. | Audience: Grade 4 to 6. | Identifiers: LCCN 2018028200 (print) | LCCN 2018031670 (ebook) | ISBN 9781541542839 (eb pdf) | ISBN 9781541501270 (lb : alk. paper)
Subjects: LCSH: Papier-mâché–Juvenile literature.
Classification: LCC TT871 (ebook) | LCC TT871 .K56 2019 (print) | DDC 745.54/2–dc23

LC record available at
https://lccn.loc.gov/2018028200

Manufactured in the United States of America
1-43797-33643-7/27/2018

MONSTER MÂCHÉ ART

BY EMILY KINGTON

HUNGRY
TOMATO™

MINNEAPOLIS

CONTENTS

MONSTER MÂCHÉ 5
TOP TIPS. 5
MATERIALS. 6
METHOD. 7

DINOSAUR MÂCHÉ. 8

MONSTER MAGNETS 10

MONSTER MATES 12

GREEDY GARBAGE MONSTER 16

MOON LIGHT 20

MONSTER BUGS 22

MONSTER TOAD 26

MUMMY IN THE CUPBOARD 28
SUPPLIES 32

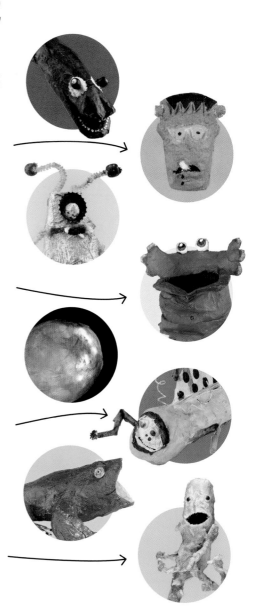

MONSTER MÂCHÉ

Papier-mâché is so much fun to do! You can make small and large models using this very simple technique.

TOP TIPS

1 Prepare different sizes of paper strips before you get sticky hands.

2 Protect surfaces from dripping paint and glue. A plastic tablecloth is great, but an old towel or piece of cardboard works well too.

3 Clean brushes in three small jars of water before using a different color of paint. Clean most of the paint off in the first jar, finish cleaning in the second jar, and store in the third jar.

4 Cover your models in a final layer of PVA glue. This will dry clear and protect the surface.

5 Use scraps of cardboard to mix your paint.

MATERIALS

CONSTRUCTION

You will need:

Masking tape Use it to shape and attach different parts of the model together.

PVA glue It's water-based, so it's easy to clean up.

Pipe cleaners Use 12 inch (30 cm) pipe cleaners.

Elastic bands and binder clips Useful for holding things in place while gluing and shaping.

Paper towel or facial tissue Use for a smooth final mâché layer and for stuffing, lining, and shaping models.

Newspaper Use for strong layers of mâché and construction.

Cotton material Use for monster mummy bandages—an old pillowcase would be ideal.

Cardboard toilet paper rolls Use for construction and making small body parts.

Cardboard Cereal boxes and wavy packing cardboard are easy to cut.

Paper clips or thin wire Use to make small accessories.

Beads

String

Plastic eyes

Magnets

Papier-mâché powder You can buy this very fine powder at most craft stores and online. You just mix with water. Use mainly for fine detail and small projects. When it dries, it's ready for painting.

Paper clay (optional) This is excellent for smaller projects and fine detail. Making it is quite time-consuming and messy, so it is best to buy this from a craft store.

Tear different sizes of paper strips before you start

METHOD

Tip: Work in one small area at a time.

1 Paste some glue onto the surface of your model.

2 Lay newspaper strips onto the glue and paste over the top of them with more glue.

3 Cover with two layers of paper and allow to dry.

4 Add a final layer of papier-mâché and then cover with strips of paper towel for a smoother finish. Leave to dry before painting. Note: Smaller projects will only need one layer of mâché.

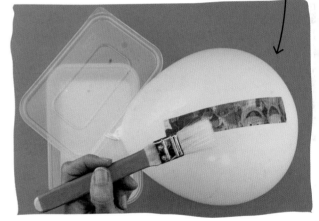

A GOOD RECIPE FOR PAPIER-MÂCHÉ GLUE

This quantity is enough to complete a number of projects, but you may have to mix the recipe twice for the larger projects. Keep leftover glue in an airtight plastic container and store in a cool place. Stir well before using again.

1 cup (237 ml) of flour

1 1/2 cups (355 ml) of water

1/2 tablespoon (7 ml) of salt (add in humid climates to prevent mold)

1 cup (237 ml) of PVA glue

1 tablespoon (15 ml) of corn flour

1 Measure out the above ingredients into a plastic bowl or container.

2 Mix together well and store in an airtight container.

DINOSAUR MÂCHÉ

MATERIALS

- Cardboard toilet paper rolls
- Balloon
- Rolled newspaper
- Newspaper strips and papier-mâché glue
- Paper towel
- Beads (optional)
- Masking tape
- PVA glue

Have you ever wanted a friendly dinosaur to sit on your shelf? Here is an easy-to-make, giant Brontosaurus!

1 Inflate the balloon, but do not fully inflate it so it is less likely to pop when masking tape is stuck on it.

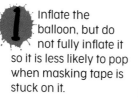

2 Cut the cardboard toilet paper rolls in half and stick them together as shown with masking tape. Attach them to the bottom of the balloon.

Neck

3 Make the neck and head of the dinosaur by rolling several layers of newspaper and taping them together.

Use masking tape to hold the shape of the neck, head, and mouth.

Head

Make the head by folding back the end and cutting the fold to make the mouth.

4 Make a tail from newspaper the same length and weight as the neck.

Attach with masking tape.

Shape the mouth with masking tape

5 Papier-mâché your dinosaur following the method on page 7.

Use larger pieces of paper on the body and smaller pieces for the neck, head and tail.

Leave to dry. If you are using beads for the eyes, glue them on before painting.

6 Paint your dinosaur and make him a friend!

MONSTER MAGNETS

These are great fun and can be given as presents—they won't take too much time to make.

MATERIALS

Mâché powder (see page 6)
Cardboard (a cereal box is perfect)
Bottle cap template
Paints
Pencil
Magnets
Small jar of clean water
PVA glue

1 Prepare the mâché powder in advance (see page 7).

2 Draw five circles onto cardboard using a round object. Copy the Frankenstein drawing by hand and cut out all of the shapes.

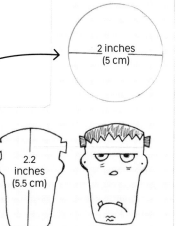

2 inches (5 cm)

2.2 inches (5.5 cm)

3 If you are going to give your Monster Magnet scary string hair, glue the hair to the round disc first and allow the glue to dry.

4 Take a small blob of the mâché powder mixture and pat it onto the round cardboard, making a domed shape. Dip your finger into the water in your jar and smooth out the surface.

Use the tip of a sharp pencil to carve out scars.

Carve out different shaped mouths.

5 Carve out eye sockets using the end of a pencil. Roll two equal amounts of mixture in the palm of your hands to make goggle eyes and pop them in the eye sockets, pressing down gently. Make sure you leave a bit of the socket showing so you can paint it a different color.

Mark the mâché with a pencil to make eyelashes or wrinkles.

Take tiny pieces of mâché, roll them in your palms, and flatten them to make spots

6 Leave to dry before painting. Paint in bright colors; paint the reverse the same color as the face and leave to dry.

For the Scar Man magnet, you may find it easier to use a fine-tip pen to color the scars black.

For the Dracula magnet, draw the hairline with a pencil before painting it black.

Carve out the Frankenstein features, hairline, eyes, and mouth, then add teeth!

7 Glue a magnet to the reverse side. Why not design some of your own? You can never have enough Monster Magnets!

These magnets are great to keep treasured photographs on your fridge

MONSTER MATES

Here is a collection of three special monsters—two friends and their small dog, Gnasher.

MATERIALS

Clothespin

Roll-on deodorant applicator or similar

Cardboard toilet paper roll

Cardboard (cereal box)

Pipe cleaner

Beads

Bottle cap

Paper towel (small strips)

Masking tape

Facial tissue

Pencil

Plastic eyes (optional—you can always paint them yourself)

Papier-mâché glue

Wire for glasses (optional)

ONE-EYE BOB

1 Using some stiff cardboard, draw around the base of the applicator. Hand draw some feet on one side of the circle, cut out the shape, and glue to the bottom of the applicator.

Glue on the bottle cap as shown

Shape the antennae and add some beads

3 Give Bob a round tummy by scrunching up some facial tissue and attaching it with masking tape. Cover the whole body and head but leave the arms and mouth free.

2 Make Bob's arms and top lip with a pipe cleaner. Make a loop and slip it over the bottle.

Use another pipe cleaner to make his antennae. Bend it in half and wind it around his arms on either side. The bend will form the bottom lip.

Scrunch small amounts of facial tissue and glue to the feet

12

4 Cover Bob in just one layer of mâché (see page 7). Do not cover the mouth and eyes. Leave Bob to dry.

5 Use some papier-mâché powder mixture (see page 6) or facial tissue dipped in the mâché glue to roll a small ball for Bob's one eye. Make some little fangs in the same way and glue them on. Once dry, Bob is ready to paint.

BOB'S FRIEND MONTY

1 To make the head and neck, make the first loop with a pipe cleaner, winding the ends together to form the neck. With the second pipe cleaner, make a loop over the top of the first one to make a sphere and wind the ends together over the neck.
   Roll a ball of tissue to fill out the sphere to form the shape of the head.

2 Flatten the cardboard toilet paper roll, draw the body shape, cut lines, and cut out the shape.
   Attach the head to the body using masking tape.

3 For the legs and arms, wind some masking tape around the pipe cleaners, paint them white, and then paint black stripes.
   For the legs, bend the painted pipe cleaner in half, bend both ends to make the feet, and tape the bended end inside the body.
   For the arms, wind the pipe cleaner around neck roughly in the middle and bend the two ends to make his hands secure with tape.

Wind a little masking tape around the hands and feet and paint a nice bright color

If you have some thin wire, give him some glasses or paint some on and make him a tie out of ribbon or string.

4 Cover Monty in papier-mâché using paper towel. Make sure you papier-mâché the inside of the body, as this will hold the head and legs in place. Paint him when dry.

GNASHER

Gnasher takes a little more time to construct, but he will make a great pet for Bob & Monty.

1 Start by making the head. Use a clothespin and wedge a bead inside to keep his mouth open. Using a cardboard toilet paper roll, cut out a neck. You can make it as long or as short as you like. Attach to the clothespin with masking tape.

Cut out some ears. Make a small bend on the straight edge to allow you to attach to the head with tape.

Cut four sets of teeth and glue onto the peg.

2 Pad out the head and neck with facial tissue to a shape that you are happy with, then cover with masking tape.

3 Now for the body and feet. Fold both of the cardboard toilet paper rolls in half as shown—one will become the feet and the other the body.

For the body, pad out the underneath with scrunched-up facial tissue and secure both ends with masking tape. Add a pipe cleaner to one end as a tail and secure with masking tape.

4 Attach the head you made earlier with tape, pad out the joint to the neck and body if needed, and cover with tape.

Attach the other folded cardboard toilet paper roll to the underneath with masking tape to form the legs.

5 When you are happy with the construction, you are ready to cover in papier-mâché. Use small strips of newspaper and given him two layers all at once.

Cover all but the teeth and inside of the mouth

6 When dry, paint Gnasher any color you like, but notice how the leg areas on this model have been shaded and how some newspaper print shows through on the head.

MONTY

GNASHER

ONE-EYE BOB

GREEDY GARBAGE MONSTER

Do you need something to throw all your trash in? Here is a great, easy-to-make monster that can collect all of your garbage and keep it off the floor!

MATERIALS

Small bucket or trash can for a template/mold (if you can't find one, don't worry—just pack a plastic bag full of newspaper to form the shape)

A large plastic bag (any plastic bag will do)

Rolls of newspaper

Cardboard

Newspaper (mâché strips)

Paper towel

PVA glue

Paint

1 For the feet and base, draw around the bottom of the trash can or bucket onto cardboard, creating a circle.

Hand draw chunky monster feet onto one side of the circle and cut out the shape.

Wavy packing cardboard is easy to use and nice and bendy

2 Measure out some cardboard that will wrap around the back of your trash can or bucket. Draw the shape shown and cut it out.

3 Place the plastic bag over the top of your trash can or bucket. Try and leave wrinkles and folds on one side because this will form the monster's saggy belly.

Use newspaper papier-mâché to cover the plastic bag, keeping the wrinkles and folds at the front.

4 Once covered, and before it's completely dry, carefully remove the trash can and stuff the inside with newspaper instead.

Turn over the top to form a lip, then use a binder clip at the front to form a "V" shape.

Leave to dry overnight and then glue the base feet onto the bottom.

5 Attach the arms, face, and eyes using masking tape.

Add tissue and padding to the feet, eyes, hands, and face.

For fuller lips, add thinly rolled newspaper using PVA glue and masking tape

6 Remove the newspaper stuffing and trim the plastic bag down. Cover the monster really well inside and out with papier-mâché using newspaper (see page 7). Cover with a final layer of paper towel inside and out and allow to dry.

GREEDY GARBAGE MONSTER

What a great place to throw your trash!

These goggle eyes are sure to follow you around the room.

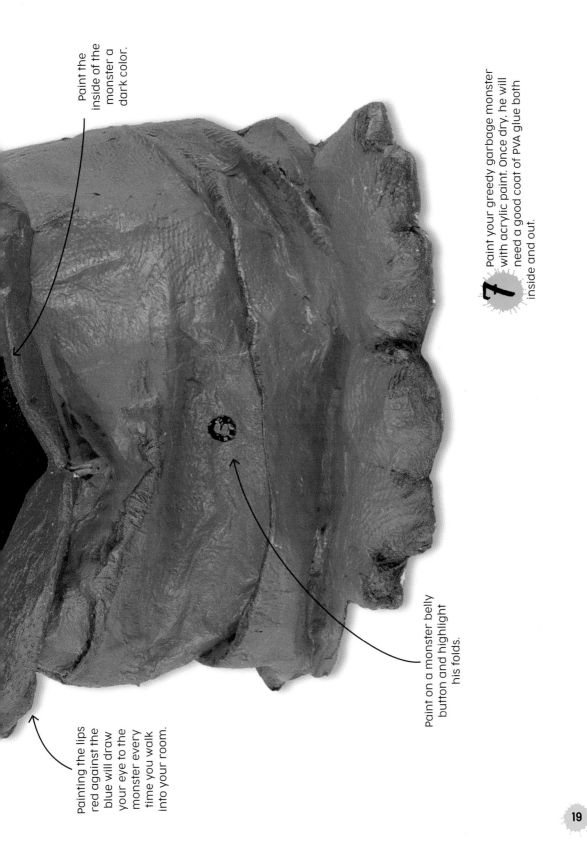

Paint the inside of the monster a dark color.

Paint your greedy garbage monster with acrylic paint. Once dry, he will need a good coat of PVA glue both inside and out.

Paint on a monster belly button and highlight his folds.

Painting the lips red against the blue will draw your eye to the monster every time you walk into your room.

MOON LIGHT

How would you like a light in your bedroom that resembles the moon and casts an eerie glow at night?

1 Partially inflate the balloon. (Do not fully inflate because doing so will make it harder to remove the balloon at the end when the mâché dries.)

2 Only use paper towel for this project because it creates a more realistic surface for the moon. Brush the surface of the balloon with mâché glue one area at a time. Cover the balloon with paper towel (you'll need about five sheets), leaving the bottom portion free. It is good to allow creases in the paper. This gives your moon craters. Leave to dry before adding a second coat.

3 Once the mâché is completely dry, pop the balloon and gently peel it away from the inside surface. Take your time because it sometimes comes away in several pieces.

4 Mix some light gray paint. If you can, use watercolor paints because you don't want it to be too dark or heavy—you are just creating a shadow effect. If you have acrylic paint, water it down and gently sponge it on in random patches.

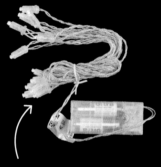

Simple battery lights can be found in a craft store or online

5 Leave to dry, then paint a thin layer of white over the top. Once dry, you can pop the lights inside. Then wait until dark before turning it on. The monster mates will look amazing in moonlight!

MONSTER BUGS

This is a fun collection of monster bugs! One can fly, one can hop, and the other disguises himself as a silent but deadly predator.

MATERIALS

Cardboard toilet paper roll
Pipe cleaners
Cardboard
Masking tape
Paper towel
Newspaper
Papier-mâché (see page 7)
Small strips of newspaper
Paints
Small piece of plastic
Paper clips
Plastic eyes (optional)
PVA glue
Thin twigs

HOPPING BUG

1 Fold the cardboard toilet paper roll in half lengthwise, secure both ends with masking tape, and trim one end to shape the tail.

2 For the head, roll some sheets of newspaper, fold them over, and attach with masking tape to the other end as shown.

For the lower jaw, cut out a small strip of cardboard and attach underneath the newspaper head.

Make two back legs

Make four front legs

3 Wind masking tape around each of the pipe cleaners, and use a pipe cleaner to shape each of the larger back legs as shown, shaping the foot at one end and leaving a small portion at the other to tape the leg to the body.

Make the four smaller legs with the remaining pipe cleaners as shown and attach to the body with masking tape.

4 Cover the body with one layer of mâché (see page 7) and leave to dry before painting.

Cut a thin strip of cardboard from the toilet paper roll to make the eyes. Roll it and squash it

FLYING BUG

1 Scrunch newspaper into a body shape. Use masking tape to get the shape you are happy with.

2 Make the legs out of pipe cleaners, using the same method as Hopping Bug.

Attach the legs to the body with masking tape.

3 Make the little wings out of plastic packaging or cardboard if you prefer. You need to bend the straight edge to allow you to glue the wing to the body.

Decorate the wing (this is easier to do before attaching to the body).

4 Make two antennae out of paper clips or thin wire. Open them out and wind around a pencil, attaching with masking tape.

5 Use the paper towel instead of newspaper for the mâché stage. Cover the bug's body.

Once dry, you can paint your bug in flying colors!

STICK INSECT

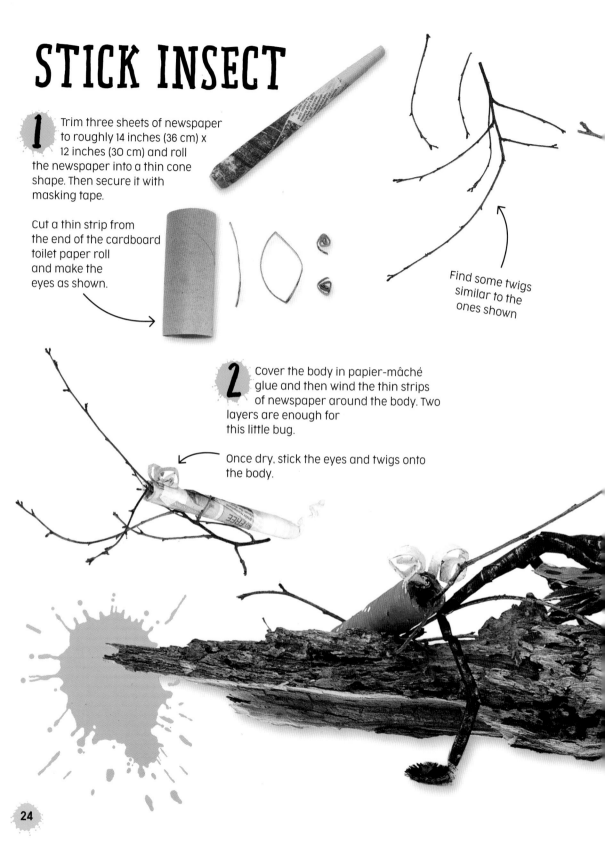

1 Trim three sheets of newspaper to roughly 14 inches (36 cm) x 12 inches (30 cm) and roll the newspaper into a thin cone shape. Then secure it with masking tape.

Cut a thin strip from the end of the cardboard toilet paper roll and make the eyes as shown.

Find some twigs similar to the ones shown

2 Cover the body in papier-mâché glue and then wind the thin strips of newspaper around the body. Two layers are enough for this little bug.

Once dry, stick the eyes and twigs onto the body.

3 Paint the stick insect in your favorite bug color!

MONSTER TOAD

If you want something on your desk to store your pens, pencils, scissors, and other essential items, how about a big, wide-mouthed toad to do the job?

MATERIALS

Large disposable coffee cup or yogurt container

Cardboard (cereal box)

Cardboard toilet paper roll

Cardboard paper towel roll

Newspaper

Masking tape

Paper towel and facial tissue

2 Pipe cleaners

Paper clips

Beads

Rubber band

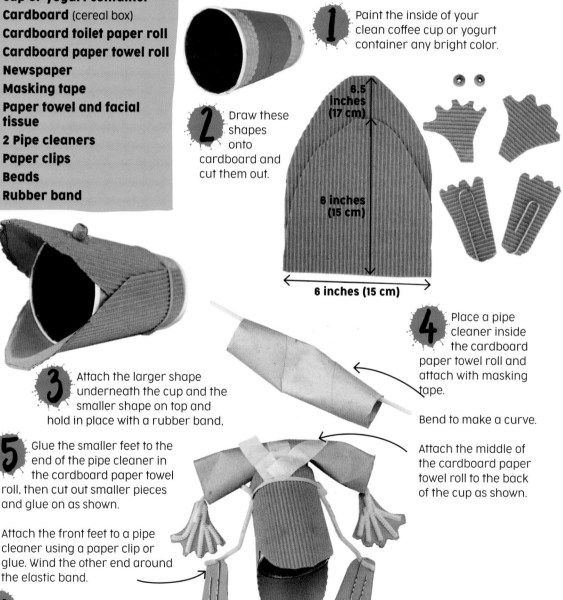

1 Paint the inside of your clean coffee cup or yogurt container any bright color.

2 Draw these shapes onto cardboard and cut them out.

6.5 inches (17 cm)

8 inches (15 cm)

6 inches (15 cm)

3 Attach the larger shape underneath the cup and the smaller shape on top and hold in place with a rubber band.

4 Place a pipe cleaner inside the cardboard paper towel roll and attach with masking tape.

Bend to make a curve.

Attach the middle of the cardboard paper towel roll to the back of the cup as shown.

5 Glue the smaller feet to the end of the pipe cleaner in the cardboard paper towel roll, then cut out smaller pieces and glue on as shown.

Attach the front feet to a pipe cleaner using a paper clip or glue. Wind the other end around the elastic band.

6 Now you will need to form the shape using facial tissue and **lots** of masking tape. Start at the head and work down to the back legs.

Wind folded pieces of paper towel around the legs and scrunch the paper up for the body until you get a nice, rounded, and well-covered toad!

Put a mound of facial tissue on top of his head to make a bump

Use lots of tape. You can add more layers on top until you are happy

7 Stick on the beads for eyes. Cut a strip of cardboard toilet paper roll as shown and wind around the beads.

8 Mâché time! Using small strips of newspaper, cover the toad completely, including inside the mouth but not inside your nicely painted cup. Follow the method explained on page 7.

9 Once the mâché is dry, paint in your own style using acrylic paints.

Instead of a pen holder, you could use him for target practice—just make some paper missiles!

MUMMY IN THE CUPBOARD
FOR THE MUMMY

1 Make an elongated head shape using two pipe cleaners. Loop one on top of the other, leaving enough at the bottom to form the neck.

2 Use facial tissue to form the inside of the head, but put less facial tissue in the bottom half to leave room for the mouth.

3 Wrap the head in masking tape, starting at the top. When you get to the mouth area, cut two strips of masking tape. Fold one edge in on itself then stick one on the top of the mouth area and one on the bottom of the mouth area. This will give the mummy an open-mouth look.

4 For the body, use three sheets of newspaper and roll into a thin cone shape. Trim to about 6 inches (13 cm) in length and secure with masking tape.
The neck beneath the mummy's head should be pushed into the thin end of the body cone and secured in place with masking tape.

5 Make two legs with pipe cleaners. Loop one end to make a foot about 1 inch (2.5 cm) long. Wrap the legs in newspaper and secure in place with some masking tape.

6 Add some arms using a pipe cleaner. Make the hands by looping each end as shown, leaving a little end piece as a thumb.

Tearing the strips of cotton creates a frayed edge

7 Soak thin strips of cotton in papier-mâché glue. Then wrap them around the entire body and head. Leave a gap for the mouth.

Leave pieces of cotton hanging for a scruffy look

8 Paint the inside of the mummy's mouth and add some plastic eyes. Finally, stain the mummy's bandages with cold tea or coffee, using a small paintbrush.

You can also make him a broom from an old paintbrush, using string and masking tape, and a little papier-mâché bucket. For the bucket, cover a plastic bottle cap with plastic wrap and papier-mâché.

MUMMY'S CUPBOARD

Make your mummy a cupboard out of stiff cardboard—it can be any size you like.

1 Take one piece of stiff cardboard, bending it at both ends to make doors and allow it to stand up. To make the doors more realistic, add panels and beads for door handles and paint the doors with acrylic paint.

2 Measure the back panel and trim some plain paper to size. Paint the background in a neutral color.
When dry, draw two shelves using a ruler and pencil as shown.

3 Draw a rack below and draw some objects hanging from hooks. You can also add some items cut out of a magazine. Add bottles and jars on the shelves. You can draw them or cut out pictures from a magazine.

Use a template to draw your jars.

Add some mice or rats for fun

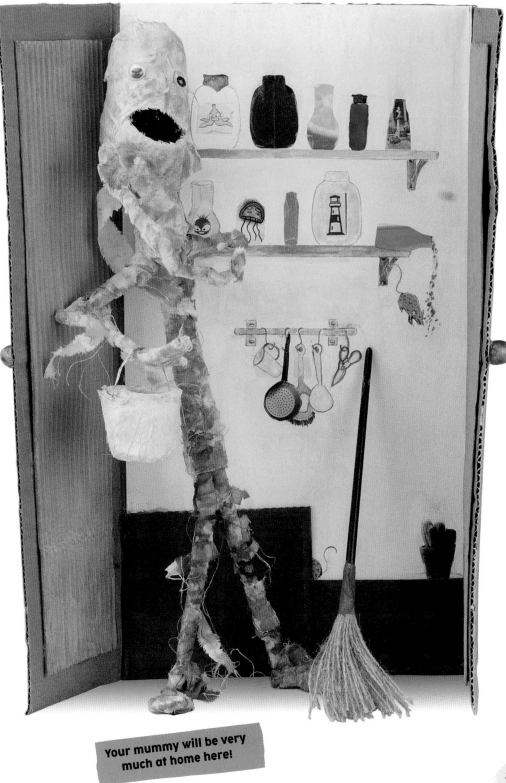

Your mummy will be very much at home here!

SUPPLIES

BRUSHES

1 brush to use specifically for glue
1 fine paintbrush for detail
2 medium paintbrushes
1 large paintbrush Use an old decorating paintbrush to mâché the larger projects,

PAINT

Acrylic paints (use for most of the projects)

Watercolor paints

USEFUL ITEMS

3 water jars for cleaning brushes
1 water jar for the glue brush
Plastic airtight container to store glue (small ice cream container or similar)
Mixing bowl for mâché (any medium plastic container)
2 Measuring cups for mâché mix (paper cups, one for the dry ingredient and one for the glue)
Pencils
Fine-tip pen
Sponge brush
Ruler
Scissors
Plain tape
Felt-tip or acrylic pens

THE AUTHOR

Emily Kington has worked in publishing and children's books for over twenty years. She loves art and is passionate about making art accessible for children and engaging them in a variety of different art forms. Emily lives in England with her husband and two children and loves outdoor sports, traveling, and good food.

FOLLOW THAT FOOD CHAIN

A CORAL REEF Food Chain

A WHO-EATS-WHAT Adventure in the Caribbean Sea

Rebecca Hogue Wojahn   Donald Wojahn

Lerner Publications Company
Minneapolis

For Eli and Cal. We hope this answers some of your questions.

There are many links in the chain that created this series. Thanks to Kristen McCurry Mohn, Carol Hinz, Danielle Carnito, Sarah Olmanson, Paul Rodeen, the staff of the L. E. Phillips Memorial Public Library, and finally, Katherine Hogue

Lerner Publications Company
A division of Lerner Publishing Group, Inc.
241 First Avenue North
Minneapolis, MN 55401 U.S.A.

Website address: www.lernerbooks.com

Library of Congress Cataloging-in-Publication Data

Wojahn, Rebecca Hogue.
  A coral reef food chain : a who-eats-what adventure in the Caribbean Sea
/ by Rebecca Hogue Wojahn and Donald Wojahn.
    p.   cm. — (Follow that food chain)
  Includes bibliographical references and index.
  ISBN 978–0–8225–7611–2 (lib. bdg. : alk. paper)
  1. Coral reef ecology—Caribbean Sea—Juvenile literature. 2. Food chains
(Ecology)—Caribbean Sea—Juvenile literature. 3. Coral reef animals—
Caribbean Sea—Juvenile literature. I. Wojahn, Donald. II. Title.
QH109.A1W65 2010
577.7'8916—dc22   2008050758

Manufactured in the United States of America
1 2 3 4 5 6 – BP – 15 14 13 12 11 10

Contents

WELCOME TO THE CORAL REEF . . . 4

CHOOSE A TERTIARY CONSUMER . . . 6

CORAL REEF PLANTS . . . 30

A CORAL REEF FOOD WEB . . . 32

GLOSSARY . . . 60

FURTHER READING AND WEBSITES . . . 61

SELECTED BIBLIOGRAPHY . . . 62

INDEX . . . 63

Introduction
WELCOME TO THE CORAL REEF

This coral reef lies hidden in the warm, shallow water just off the shore of a Caribbean island. From the beach, waves gently roll over calm water. But duck your head under the waves, and you'll see an underwater jungle full of life.

Coral cliffs and ledges of every color and shape overlap in the clear, blue water off the edge of the island. Star coral, flower coral, table coral, staghorn coral, mushroom coral, brain coral, leather coral, organ pipe coral, sea whips, and sea fans—their names alone describe the textures and variety. Schools of brightly colored fish dart over and under and through the coral reef. Spiny and slimy creatures of every size and shape cling to the surfaces of it. The reef is a whirling maze of color and life.

Coral reefs grow in warm, shallow waters of the ocean, usually just offshore. Coral reefs only take up 1 percent of all the space in the ocean. Yet 25 percent of all ocean life lives in them. The longer you look, the more life you see. Get ready to meet some of the million coral reef creatures.

UNITED STATES

ATLANTIC OCEAN

Gulf of Mexico

CUBA

HAITI

PUERTO RICO

JAMAICA

Caribbean Sea

CENTRAL AMERICA

SOUTH AMERICA

N

The Coral Reef Habitat

The coral reef habitat is made up of the rocklike skeletal structures of tiny animals called coral. A network of sponges, rocks, and plants on the ocean floor are also a part of the habitat.

Choose a
TERTIARY CONSUMER

All the living things in the coral reef are necessary for its health and survival. From the tiger shark cruising through the coral towers to the fingerprint snail stuck to the stones, the living things are all connected. Animals and other organisms feed on and transfer energy to one another. This is called a **food chain** or a **food web**.

In food chains, the strongest **predators** are called **tertiary consumers**. They hunt other animals for food and have few natural enemies. Some of the animals they eat are called **secondary consumers**. Secondary consumers are also predators. They hunt plant-eating animals. Plant eaters are **primary consumers**.

Plants are **producers**. Using energy from the sun, they produce their own food. Plants take in **nutrients** from the water. They also provide nutrients to the animals that eat them.

Decomposers are creatures or bacteria that break down dead plants and animals. Decomposers change them into the nutrients found in the water.

The plants and animals in a food chain depend on one another. Sometimes there's a break in the chain, such as one type of animal dying out. This loss ripples through the rest of the **habitat**.

Begin your journey through the coral reef food web by choosing a large **carnivore**, or meat eater. These tertiary consumers are at the top of the food chain. That means that, for the most part, they don't have any enemies in the ocean.

When it's time for the tertiary consumer to eat, pick its meal and flip to that page. As you go through the book, don't be surprised if you backtrack and end up where you never expected to be. That's how food webs work—they're complicated. And watch out for those dead ends! When you hit one of those, you have to go back to page 7 and start over with another tertiary consumer.

The main role a plant or animal plays in the coral reef food web is identified by a color-coded shape. Here is the key to that code:

TERTIARY CONSUMER

PRODUCER

SECONDARY CONSUMER

PRIMARY CONSUMER

DECOMPOSER

7

To choose . . .

. . . a tiger shark. TURN TO PAGE 8.
. . . a great barracuda. TURN TO PAGE 22.
. . . a spotted moray eel. TURN TO PAGE 40.
. . . a smalltooth sawfish. TURN TO PAGE 33.

To learn more about a coral reef food web, GO TO PAGE 32.

TIGER SHARK *(Galeocerdo cuvier)*

The dark gray tiger shark slides past the far edge of the reef. She's as long as a minivan, and since she's full grown, her tiger markings faded years ago. As she propels herself with her tail, she cracks open her mouth. Water spills into it, rushes past her gills, and then out the five gill slits on her sides. She has special slits above her eyes too. They bring the **oxygen** in the water directly to her eyes and brain.

It's getting darker. She'll need her eyesight and other senses to hunt in the dark. She slips from the deep waters of the ocean into the shallows of the reef. She listens for the low noise of a fish in trouble. Her sense of smell is one of her best hunting features, though. She can smell a drop of blood in the water from more than a quarter mile (0.4 kilometers) away!

Except for great white sharks, tiger sharks are responsible for the most attacks on humans. The best way to avoid sharks is to not swim at dusk or dawn. That's when sharks are the most active in shallow water. About twenty-five to thirty human deaths by sharks are reported each year. On the other hand, humans are responsible for millions of shark deaths each year.

But there's no blood in the water tonight. So she trusts her sixth sense—her **electrosense**. She can feel the weak electrical signals living things give off. She roots in the sand with her snout, uncovering a lobster. It scurries away. As she follows it, she comes across something she doesn't recognize. It doesn't matter to her that she doesn't know what it is. With her multiple rows of sawlike teeth, she rips into it. She twists and shakes it so hard that some of her teeth pull out and sprinkle in the sand. It's okay—new ones are growing all the time.

She gulps down chunks. But just as she gets them down, her stomach turns. It seems her meal doesn't want to stay down. She slows. With a heave, she spits up what she just swallowed—the shredded remains of a beach towel. The towel drifts back down to the ocean floor. Things stay remarkably preserved in her stomach. That's because her stomach has no digestive juices to break things down. It's more of a holding place for her body to decide to keep or get rid of what she's swallowed.

Her stomach is empty again. The shark circles around and catches sight of a turtle. She curls her body and bumps the turtle once or twice with her nose. The turtle paddles furiously, but the tiger shark has at last found dinner. That hard shell barely slows her down.

Her meal will last her a few days. *Last week for dinner, the tiger shark chomped . . .*

. . . a southern stingray skimming through the water. To see what another stingray is up to, TURN TO PAGE 24.

. . . a trumpetfish hiding in the weeds. To see what another trumpetfish is up to, TURN TO PAGE 20.

. . . a queen triggerfish that didn't hide in the coral quickly enough. To see what another queen triggerfish is up to, TURN TO PAGE 42.

. . . a young great barracuda too busy looking for its own meal. To see what another great barracuda is up to, TURN TO PAGE 22.

. . . a queen parrot fish pecking at the coral. To see what another queen parrot fish is up to, TURN TO PAGE 34.

. . . a newly hatched hawksbill turtle. To see what another hawksbill is up to, TURN TO PAGE 58.

. . . a sharpnose puffer fish darting through the shallow water. To see what another sharpnose puffer fish is up to, TURN TO PAGE 48.

. . . a Caribbean monk seal playing in the waves. To see what another monk seal is up to, TURN TO PAGE 57.

FOUREYE BUTTERFLYFISH (*Chaetodon capistratus*)

The foureye butterflyfish hovers motionless over a sea anemone. Then, with a quick dart, the butterflyfish nabs one of the anemone's **tentacles** with her fine bristle teeth.

Nearby, her mate is nibbling too. They've been together for two years and are never far from each other. Their bodies are perfectly shaped for the darting, twisting, and reversing that are needed to quickly grab their food.

They also need to be able to make fast getaways. A small reef shark swishes over the coral overhang, his fins down, looking for a meal. In an instant, the area is deserted of butterflyfish. They cower in the nooks and crannies of the corals, sponges, and stones.

As the shark moves on, the butterflyfish creeps back out from her hiding place—but wait! Where is her mate? She swims in a circle, looking. Did the shark get him? She swims faster, up to the top of the coral, scanning for him. Up here, she's got an amazing view of the busy world of the reef. Fish and colors swirl below her. But she's looking for a particular one.

There, down below, finally! Her mate! He's been looking for her too. They speed toward each other and spin in circles as if they're dancing. It's good to have a friend on the reef.

Last night for dinner, the butterflyfish pair ate . . .

. . . **tiny coral polyps.** To see what a group of coral polyps is up to, TURN TO PAGE 44.

. . . **a giant Caribbean sea anemone, before it got too giant.** To see what another sea anemone is up to, TURN TO PAGE 54.

. . . **coral.** To see what a group of coral is up to, TURN TO PAGE 46.

. . . **a fan worm on the bottom of the reef.** To see what another fan worm is up to, TURN TO PAGE 38.

. . . **pieces of sponges.** To see what another sponge is up to, TURN TO PAGE 36.

. . . **plankton drifting in the current.** To see what other plankton are up to, TURN TO PAGE 18.

REMORA
(Echeneis naucrates)

The remora waggles her narrow tail and scoots through the water. This fish— also known as a shark sucker—is swimming solo. But usually she prefers to hitch a ride on faster creatures. Remoras don't have air bladders inside that help them to stay up or down in the water, so they're not very good swimmers. As she weaves her way through the reef, she's on the lookout.

Ah, there! A huge manta ray, as wide across as a dinner table, powers across the water above. Like a giant underwater bat, the ray blocks out the sunlight for a moment. The remora chases after him. As the manta ray slows, the remora glides under him. On top of her head is a flat sucking disk. It allows her to grab onto things. She aims and latches onto the white belly of the ray. Oh, that's better. The remora can just relax and go along for the ride.

The manta ray doesn't shake the remora loose. The ray knows the remora will help out in her own way. Already, the remora has nibbled off a few **parasites** from the underside of the manta ray. The ray swoops low for a snack of scallops. As he crunches into them, the remora picks through the leftovers that float in the water.

Last night for dinner, the remora gobbled down bits of...

Hitchhiking Remoras

Remoras don't always swim with another animal. Often they can be seen traveling alone in the reef. But they are most known for seeking out other large swimmers and tagging along. In fact, fishers used to use this to their advantage. The fishers would tie lines to remoras and release them into the deep. Most times, the remoras would find a ray, shark, or turtle. Then, once the remora attached itself, the fisher would pull him in—along with the hefty host fish.

. . . a spotted moray eel caught out of his den. To see what another moray eel is up to, TURN TO PAGE 40.

. . . a queen parrot fish with a damaged fin. To see what another queen parrot fish is up to, TURN TO PAGE 34.

. . . a small southern stingray. To see what another stingray is up to, TURN TO PAGE 24.

. . . a sharpnose puffer fish exploring the reef. To see what another sharpnose puffer fish is up to, TURN TO PAGE 48.

. . . a foureye butterflyfish looking for his mate. To see what another butterflyfish is up to, TURN TO PAGE 12.

. . . a young great barracuda that swam out a little too deep. To see what another great barracuda is up to, TURN TO PAGE 22.

. . . a queen triggerfish flitting through the water. To see what another queen triggerfish is up to, TURN TO PAGE 42.

ANTILLEAN SCALLOP *(Bractechlamys antillarum)*

The delicate fan-shaped shell of the Antillean scallop creaks open. The inside of the scallop is soft and muscular compared to his protective shell. The scallop opens wide, waiting for plankton—tiny bits of plants and animals—to float in. When they do, tiny hairs on the scallop move the food down to his mouth and then stomach.

But this meal is interrupted. A stingray swims into the area. For a moment, the ray's shadow passes over the scallop. That change in light is enough to alert the scallop to danger. The scallop slams his shell shut. He closes so quickly that the water rushing out of him pushes his shell backward. The ray follows, and the scallop opens and closes again, scooting away. It is the scallop's only way of escaping. This time he has pushed himself under a ledge of table coral. The ray pokes him for a bit and then swims off in search of something easier to trap.

Maybe this is a good place to stay for a while. The scallop sticks out his foot, a soft muscular part of his body, and starts to burrow in the sand. Soon he has buried himself. The only clue that the scallop is there is the small hole in the sand he uses to breathe water. The rest of the reef bustles on as the scallop takes a break.

Last night for dinner, the scallop ate . . .

Trouble in the Food Chain

Scallops are getting rarer in the Atlantic Ocean. But it's not because of a problem directly affecting them. It's because of the sharks. Sharks like to eat stingrays, and stingrays like to eat scallops. But sharks have been overfished, and there are far fewer of them than in the past. Fewer sharks mean more stingrays. And more stingrays mean more scallops being eaten.

...more plankton. To see what other plankton are up to, TURN TO PAGE 18.

PLANKTON

The huge mouth of the whale shark sucks down his meal. You'd think something so huge would be after a much larger prey, but he's not. The whale shark is after some of the smallest bits in the ocean—tiny plankton.

The waters of the coral reef are warm and shallow. That's the best environment for plankton. Plankton include bits of **algae**, and mollusk, snail, and sea star **larvas**. Even those Portuguese man-of-wars floating in the currents are plankton. That's right—not all plankton is tiny. Any living creature that floats and drifts in the ocean is plankton. That means that even some larger animals, such as jellyfish, are plankton.

Phytoplankton Rule

All plants—trees, flowers, weeds, and phytoplankton—take in carbon dioxide and give off oxygen. But can you guess which plants change the most carbon dioxide to oxygen? Not the towering redwoods or the dense rain forest jungles. No, it is the tiny phytoplankton in the oceans.

But scientists are concerned about phytoplankton. They worry that the warming temperatures of Earth might kill off the tiny sea plants. That would mean trouble for all living things, which depend on the oxygen phytoplankton produce.

A Portuguese man-of-war floats in the Caribbean.

No matter what size they are, **phytoplankton** or **zooplankton** drift together. Phytoplankton, such as diatoms and algae, are tiny plants. They float in the shallow water so that they can absorb the sunlight and create **oxygen**. Zooplankton are animals that breathe oxygen and eat. Some, such as copepods, are plankton their entire lives. Others, such as sea star and mollusk larvas, are plankton for a time but will grow up to be something else. Without these creatures, the entire food chain of the ocean would crumble.

Last night for dinner, the plankton took in nutrients from . . .

. . . a dead tiger shark. To see what another tiger shark is up to, TURN TO PAGE 8.

. . . a dead giant Caribbean sea anemone. To see what another sea anemone is up to, TURN TO PAGE 54.

. . . a dead spotted moray eel. To see what another moray eel is up to, TURN TO PAGE 40.

. . . dead sponges. To see what another sponge is up to, TURN TO PAGE 36.

. . . a dead remora. To see what another remora is up to, TURN TO PAGE 14.

. . . a dead hawksbill turtle. To see what another hawksbill is up to, TURN TO PAGE 58.

. . . a dead great barracuda. To see what another great barracuda is up to, TURN TO PAGE 22.

. . . a dead Caribbean monk seal. To see what another monk seal is up to, TURN TO PAGE 57.

TRUMPETFISH *(Aulostomus maculatus)*

A school of trumpetfish snoozes in the eelgrass. The group sleeps with their noses to the seabed and their tails pointing up toward the water's surface. They look just like brown sticks in the weeds. But as the sun hits the reef, the trumpetfish start to stir. And they aim their long, skinny bodies in different directions to hunt on their own.

One trumpetfish flicks along the surface for a while. Then she spies what she's been looking for. It's a blue tang heading for a cleaning station, where other fish will eat the parasites off his scales. The trumpetfish glides up quietly next to the tang. Her scales turn from brown to vivid blue. She can change colors when she needs to. She cozies up to the tang. It's called shadow stalking. She's hoping no one will notice her.

A trumpetfish shadow stalks a queen parrot fish.

The tang presents himself to the cleaner fish, opening his mouth and spreading his fins wide. And that's when the trumpetfish strikes. Darting out and around, the trumpetfish ambushes a cleaner fish. She sucks it into her huge mouth. Even though he is wider than she is, her jaws unhinge and expand, just as some snakes' jaws do.

The other fish at the cleaning station have disappeared. But the trumpetfish leaves with a satisfying bulge in her belly.

Last night for dinner, the trumpetfish sucked down . . .

. . . **a tiny queen parrot fish in the shallows.** To see what another parrot fish is up to, TURN TO PAGE 34.

. . . **a banded coral shrimp.** To see what another shrimp is up to, TURN TO PAGE 52.

. . . **a sharpnose puffer fish before it can puff up.** To see what another sharpnose puffer fish is up to, TURN TO PAGE 48.

. . . **an Antillean scallop.** To see what another scallop is up to, TURN TO PAGE 16.

. . . **a remora having trouble swimming in the current.** To see what another remora is up to, TURN TO PAGE 14.

. . . **a foureye butterflyfish at a cleaning station.** To see what another butterflyfish is up to, TURN TO PAGE 12.

. . . **an ambushed queen triggerfish.** To see what another queen triggerfish is up to, TURN TO PAGE 42.

GREAT BARRACUDA *(Sphyraena barracuda)*

Zip! A silver flash speeds through the water. It's a great barracuda. He's as long as you are and slender and strong.

The barracuda spies his next meal sinking toward the sandy bottom. He circles around. His **prey** doesn't seem to notice.

The barracuda bursts toward his victim. He hits it at 36 miles (58 kilometers) per hour—faster than cars travel on most city streets. His mouth, meant for tearing, closes around the prey. But wait. What's this? The barracuda spits out his mouthful. What he thought was a shiny fish was just a wristwatch, dropped overboard from a boat above.

The barracuda circles around again. Ah, he spies a nice fat squid. The barracuda tears toward it. The squid doesn't have a chance. The long bottom jaw of the barracuda is studded with piercing teeth.

The squid is too big for the barracuda to swallow in one bite. So the barracuda clamps down and, with a hard shake, pulls a chunk from it. The rest of the squid drifts down. But seconds later, the barracuda's at it again. After this meal, he'll be set for days.

Last night for dinner, the barracuda stalked down . . .

Don't Order the Barracuda

With their fearsome mouthful of teeth, barracudas scare many people. Swimmers are afraid of coming across barracudas in the water. But barracudas rarely attack people. If they do, it's usually because the person is holding a speared fish or is wearing something shiny, such as a bracelet.

But eating a barracuda is dangerous to humans. Like many reef fish, barracudas have a poison called ciguatoxin. Ciguatoxin naturally occurs in smaller reef animals. Because barracudas are at the top of the reef food chain and eat lots of smaller fish, the ciguatoxin builds up in their systems. When humans eat barracuda meat, they also eat the poison, and it can make them very sick.

. . . a sharpnose puffer fish that turned the wrong corner. To see what another puffer fish is up to, **TURN TO PAGE 48.**

. . . a spotted moray eel swimming between holes in the coral. To see what another moray eel is up to, **TURN TO PAGE 40.**

. . . a trumpetfish stalking a cleaning station. To see what another trumpetfish is up to, **TURN TO PAGE 20.**

. . . a southern stingray sailing through the water. To see what another stingray is up to, **TURN TO PAGE 24.**

. . . a Caribbean monk seal cub that strayed too deep. To see what another monk seal is up to, **TURN TO PAGE 57.**

. . . a queen triggerfish out for a bite to eat. To see what another triggerfish is up to, **TURN TO PAGE 42.**

. . . a smalltooth sawfish out looking for its own meal. To see what another sawfish is up to, **TURN TO PAGE 33.**

. . . a remora knocked off a manta ray. To see what another remora is up to, **TURN TO PAGE 14.**

SOUTHERN STINGRAY *(Dasyatis americana)*

A hermit crab jumps aside as the sand under him starts to shake. A southern stingray ripples his fins and shrugs away the sand of his resting place. The crab scuttles away before the stingray sees him. With powerful flaps of his fins, the ray glides through the clear water. He sweeps low and traps a garden eel under his wide, kitelike body. Keeping the eel under him, he scoots forward. His mouth is on the bottom of his body. When his mouth is right over the eel, the ray crunches into it with sharp teeth.

After his snack, he heads to the local cleaning station. Leeches constantly worm their way into his rough skin. He aims toward a school of cleaner wrasse fish. He holds still as they pinch and pluck and nibble the worms and leeches off him. They love the free meal, and the stingray stays healthy because of it. If he doesn't get them removed once in a while, the leeches would make him sick.

Without warning, the wrasses scatter and disappear. The stingray turns to see a shadow pass overhead—a large shadow with a wide, flat head—a hammerhead shark!

The ray flicks his fins to escape, but the shark has spotted him. As it draws nearer, the ray raises his long spiny tail. On the end is a dangerous barb. The shark darts in for a grab, and the ray snaps his tail. The barb catches the shark right between the eyes. It injects poison into the shark. The shark flinches. The jab and the poison distract him just long enough for the stingray to take off.

The barb on the end of a stingray's tail

Killer Cousin

Sharks and stingrays are actually related. They both have skeletons made from cartilage. Cartilage is a soft, bendable material—like the stuff your ears and the inside of your nose are made of. Sharks and stingrays also have similar skin. It's made of small toothlike scales called dermal denticles. And like stingrays, sharks have electrosense. A shark won't hesitate to use electrosense to hunt down a ray for dinner. Just because sharks are related to rays doesn't mean they won't eat them.

The stingray glides low over the sandy bottom to catch his breath. He pulls water in through vents behind his eyes called spiracles. The ray's body takes **oxygen** from the water. Then the water gushes back out through gill slits on the bottom of his body.

As he glides, he's also hunting. He has **electrosense**—the ability to feel the weak electrical fields that all animals give out. The ray's electrosense helps him to find food under the sand. He slows and flaps his fins. The sand stirs up just enough that he's able to pin down a buried clam. Gulp!

Last night for dinner, the southern stingray hunted . . .

. . . a young spotted moray eel looking for a new home. To see what another moray eel is up to, TURN TO PAGE 40.

. . . a long-horn nudibranch rolling in the waves. To see what another nudibranch is up to, TURN TO PAGE 28.

. . . an Antillean scallop. To see what another scallop is up to, TURN TO PAGE 16.

. . . a banded coral shrimp or two. To see what another shrimp is up to, TURN TO PAGE 52.

LONG-HORN NUDIBRANCH (*Austraeolis catina*)

The long-horn nudibranch—sometimes called a sea slug—slowly slides along the edge of the organ pipe coral. Its head **tentacles** quiver, tasting the water. The tentacles do more than just taste. The nudibranch also uses them to smell and feel its way around.

Not that the nudibranch does a lot of traveling. It's content to move at a pace that'd be barely noticeable to you. It creeps up to a sponge and begins feeding.

Nudibranches may not move fast, but they are noticeable in a different way. They have bright colors and textures. Brilliant featherlike parts and horns of every color and pattern grow on the backs of nudibranches. Nudibranches soak up colors from the food they eat.

They also soak up poisons from their food. The poisons don't hurt them, but they do make the nudibranches taste bad to their predators.

The nudibranch inches along. It nudges up against another long-horn. Every nudibranch is both male and female. But each one still needs another nudibranch to create more nudibranches. If these two remain near each other, they will create **larvas**. The larvas will float off in the sea to find new homes and grow into new nudibranches.

Last night for dinner, the long-horn nudibranch munched on . . .

... plankton. To see what other plankton are up to, TURN TO PAGE 18.

... coral polyps. To see what a group of coral polpys is up to, TURN TO PAGE 44.

... algae. To see what the plants of the coral reef are like, TURN TO PAGE 30.

... coral. To see what a group of coral is up to, TURN TO PAGE 46.

... sponges. To see what another sponge is up to, TURN TO PAGE 36.

... a giant Caribbean sea anemone. To see what another sea anemone is up to, TURN TO PAGE 54.

... a fan worm. To see what another fan worm is up to, TURN TO PAGE 38.

CORAL REEF PLANTS

As you glide through the coral reef, you'll notice there aren't a lot of plants. But if you look closely, you'll see plants tucked away among the lumps and bumps of coral. Those plants play an important role in the reef.

Sea grass

Sea grass grows along the ocean floor. Waving in the ocean's current, sea grass looks just like a field of tall grass. It even has flowers. Sea grass is the only blooming ocean plant. In some places, the sea grass meadows are so big and thick that you can see them beneath the water all the way from up in space.

Drifting through the water are long strands of **marine algae**, or seaweed. Many are longer than you are! These algae come in blue green, red, green, and brown. These tangled masses that float through the ocean are very important to the ocean's survival. They provide the **oxygen** that many of the sea animals need. But, on the other hand, too much algae can kill the coral reef by blocking out its sunlight and nutrients. Like the rest of the habitat, the plants of the coral reef depend on a delicate balance.

Last night for dinner, the plants took in nutrients from . . .

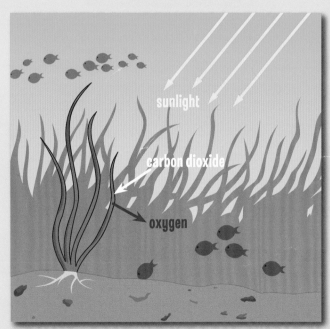

sunlight

carbon dioxide

oxygen

Plants make food and oxygen through photosynthesis. Plants draw in carbon dioxide (a gas found in air) and water. Then they use the energy from sunlight to turn the carbon dioxide and water into their food.

. . . a dead great barracuda.
To see what another
great barracuda is up to,
TURN TO PAGE 22.

. . . a dead tiger shark.
To see what another
tiger shark is up to,
TURN TO PAGE 8.

. . . a dead hawksbill turtle. To
see what another hawksbill
is up to, TURN TO PAGE 58.

**. . . a dead southern
stingray.** To see what
another stingray is
up to, TURN TO PAGE 24.

**. . . a dead foureye
butterflyfish.** To
see what another
butterflyfish is up
to, TURN TO PAGE 12.

. . . a dead trumpetfish.
To see what another
trumpetfish is up to,
TURN TO PAGE 20.

**. . . a dead Caribbean
monk seal.** To see what
another monk seal is
up to, TURN TO PAGE 57.

**. . . a dead smalltooth
sawfish.** To see what
another sawfish is up
to, TURN TO PAGE 33.

A CORAL REEF FOOD WEB

In the coral reef, energy moves around the food chain from the sun to plants, from plants to plant eaters, and from animals to the creatures that eat them. Energy also moves from dead animals to the plants and animals that draw nutrients from them.

SMALLTOOTH SAWFISH *(Pristis pectinata)*

The smalltooth sawfish lurks near the bottom in the shallows near the reef. As he grows hungrier, he twitches his sharklike body into action. Aiming for a school of fish, he slashes his "saw." He spears the fish with the teeth on the outside edges of his snout. Then he scrapes their bodies off on the seafloor and gobbles them up. The only problem is, the smalltooth sawfish isn't doing much of this anymore. In fact, it is in danger of becoming **extinct**. That's right, this is a ***DEAD END***. Smalltooth sawfish have been overfished and are hard to find in the waters of the Caribbean.

Bottom Trawlers Banned

One of the threats to the smalltooth sawfish is bottom trawling fishing. That is when fishers drag miles and miles of weighted nets across the seafloor. The fish get caught in the nets and die. But bottom trawling harms more than just the smalltooth sawfish. It breaks up coral, uproots underwater plants, and snags dolphins, sharks, and turtles. Basically, it scours the ocean floor of life and leaves it broken and ruined. Most countries have banned this kind of fishing, but it still goes on illegally. And it's still putting animals

QUEEN PARROT FISH *(Scarus vetula)*

Crunch! Crunch! The queen parrot fish can be heard yards away as he scrapes at the coral with his beaklike teeth. He breaks off a piece and swallows it down. He doesn't really want the coral, though. What he's really after are the **algae** and sponges inside and on it.

Once he swallows the hard parts, the bits of coral and rocks are ground up into tiny sandy bits inside of him. Then he digests the algae and gets rid of the sand. That's right—some of the sand you walk on at a tropical beach was probably pooped out by parrot fish. One parrot fish can make 100 pounds (45 kilograms) of coral sand a year!

The water's growing dimmer as the sun sets. Since this parrot fish is still small enough to worry about predators, he begins looking for a place to rest for the night. He tucks himself in a crevice in the stone and begins blowing a cloud of **mucus** from his mouth. It flows around his body until he is all covered. There's a hole in the mucus cloud for him to take in water and breathe. Another hole at the back lets the water flow out. With his mucus envelope keeping him safe, he drifts off.

Last night for dinner, the parrot fish munched...

A queen parrot fish protects itself with a mucus envelope.

Male, Female, or Supermale?

Queen parrot fish go through many stages as they grow older. They start out as males and females that are gray with white stripes. They change to dark gray as young adults. As they grow up, some become adult females or adult males. Others go on to become "supermales." Supermales are extra colorful and often lead a group of female fish. But, even stranger, not all grown-up males were born male. Sometimes a female will become male as she grows.

. . . sponges tucked in the coral. To see what another sponge is up to, TURN TO PAGE 36.

. . . a black sea urchin creeping along an organ pipe coral. To see what another sea urchin is up to, TURN TO PAGE 50.

. . . plankton drifting in the water. To see what other plankton are up to, TURN TO PAGE 18.

. . . a fan worm waving in the current. To see what another fan worm is up to, TURN TO PAGE 38.

. . . coral polyps. To see what a group of coral polyps is up to, TURN TO PAGE 44.

. . . coral. To see what a group of coral is up to, TURN TO PAGE 46.

. . . algae growing in the coral. To see what the plants of the coral reef are like, TURN TO PAGE 30.

SPONGE (Porifera)

The sponges hold tight to the coral. They're all shapes and sizes—tiny tubes, huge vases, delicate branches and stems, and giant wedges that look like elephant ears. That enormous barrel sponge over there is big enough for you to stand in. It has been growing for almost a thousand years.

Tube sponges

The water rushes through the tiny holes and tunnels all over the barrel sponge's body. Tiny bits of plants and animals called plankton are soaked into the sponge. Plankton give the sponge nutrients. Even though it doesn't have a heart, brain, or blood, sponges are animals, not plants. That's because they eat and breathe **oxygen** in the water.

Swooping over the reef, a hawksbill turtle stops for a meal. Crunch! Its hard beak tears into the nutrient-filled sponge. Behind it, crabs and shrimp move in to feast on the insides of the sponge that the turtle has cracked open. A crab rips a tiny bit off and scuttles away. But instead of eating it, he crawls under it. It's almost a perfect disguise. The crab gets a hiding place, and eventually the sponge will start to grow—stuck tight to the crab's hard shell like a little hat. Meanwhile, the sponge has already begun healing itself. It will eventually grow back the broken part.

Last night for dinner, the sponge soaked up . . .

Red erect rope sponges, orange elephant ear sponge, and lavender rope sponges

36

Sponges Can Be Sharp!

Your kitchen sponge is named after the natural sponges found in the reef. But not all ocean sponges are soft. Some do have squishy skeletons that have been harvested for washing and padding for thousands of years. (The ancient Romans used them for toilet paper!) But some are made of a bonylike material that makes the sponges hard like coral. Other sponges are like glass—they are brittle and sharp and will cut anything that touches them.

. . . plankton floating in the water. To see what other plankton are up to, TURN TO PAGE 18.

. . . algae drifting in the ocean. To see what the plants of the coral reef are like, TURN TO PAGE 30.

FAN WORM *(Sabellida)*
AND OTHER DECOMPOSERS

The cluster of fan worms clings to the stone. Small circles of featherlike fans ripple in the ocean's current. These fans are more than just decoration. Water flows through them, and each feathery circle traps food in the water. But it's not fish or even bits of **algae** that the fan worms are eating. They are after the tiny bits of dead animals and plants in the water. Without fan worms and other decomposers, such as bacteria, the ocean would soon be clogged and full of dead matter. Fan worms and other decomposers help to filter and clean the water for the other animals of the reef.

Last night for dinner, the fan worms slurped bits of...

. . . a dead tiger shark. To see what another tiger shark is up to, TURN TO PAGE 8.

. . . dead sponges. To see what another sponge is up to, TURN TO PAGE 36.

. . . a dead hawksbill turtle. To see what another hawksbill is up to, TURN TO PAGE 58.

. . . a dead Caribbean monk seal. To see what another monk seal is up to, TURN TO PAGE 57.

. . . a dead queen triggerfish. To see what another queen triggerfish is up to, TURN TO PAGE 42.

. . . a dead southern stingray. To see what another stingray is up to, TURN TO PAGE 24.

. . . a dead queen parrot fish. To see what another queen parrot fish is up to, TURN TO PAGE 34.

. . . dead algae. To see what the plants of the coral reef are like, TURN TO PAGE 30.

SPOTTED MORAY EEL *(Gymnothorax moringa)*

As the sun fades from the reef, the spotted moray eel stirs in her lair. She may look like a snake, but she's a fish—a long fish, as long and as thick as your leg. She doesn't have side fins as other fish do. But she does have a long top fin that runs the length of her body. This and her tail fin steer her through the water. But she doesn't need to swim much. She tends to wait for her food from the safety of her hideaway.

Slowly, she extends her narrow head out from under the coral ledge where she hides by day. She keeps most of her body tucked away. The top of her moves gently in the waves. She opens her mouth wide, and her sharp teeth gleam. Then she closes her mouth. She opens and closes her mouth again and again. This is how she forces water past her gills so she can breathe.

Suddenly, she lunges and snaps her jaws shut. An unlucky goby fish is trapped in her jaws. There's little chance of escape. Already, the eel's second set of jaws at the back of her throat have closed around the little fish. These jaws pull the fish down her long throat. And the eel waits for another passerby.

Last night for dinner, the eel caught . . .

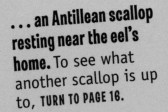

. . . an Antillean scallop resting near the eel's home. To see what another scallop is up to, TURN TO PAGE 16.

. . . a black sea urchin sliding along the coral. To see what another sea urchin is up to, TURN TO PAGE 50.

. . . a banded coral shrimp caught in a current that drifted too close to the eel. To see what another shrimp is up to, TURN TO PAGE 52.

. . . a long-horn nudibranch near the ocean floor. To see what another nudibranch is up to, TURN TO PAGE 28.

QUEEN TRIGGERFISH (Balistes vetula)

The queen triggerfish watches over her nest. Last night she and her mate used their fins to clean an area on the reef's floor. Then she laid her eggs in the shallow dip they had created. The pair guards the eggs in the nest. Their snapping, sharp teeth frighten away many that try to stop by for a snack.

The male triggerfish swims around the reef. He's hungry. He scoots in close to a spiny sea urchin. The stinging barbs don't scare him off. The triggerfish uses his long snout to aim a quick puff of water at the urchin. The puff spins the urchin off its perch. It lands on the coral below. Another puff flips the urchin over. Then the sharp spines don't matter. The triggerfish dives for the soft parts on the exposed bottom of the urchin. He munches away—right around the spines.

The light is fading from the reef. The triggerfish returns to the nest. He and his mate find narrow spaces in the coral nearby. They tuck themselves in for the night by wedging the spines on their upper fins into the coral. Even if a predator spies them, it can't pull them out of the coral. They are safe until morning.

Last night for dinner, the triggerfish gulped down . . .

. . . **a black sea urchin, spines and all.** To see what another sea urchin is up to, TURN TO PAGE 50.

. . . **a banded coral shrimp crawling across a brain coral.** To see what another shrimp is up to, TURN TO PAGE 52.

. . . **an Antillean scallop.** To see what another scallop is up to, TURN TO PAGE 16.

. . . **a giant Caribbean sea anemone he pulled from the coral.** To see what another sea anemone is up to, TURN TO PAGE 54.

. . . **a long-horn nudibranch creeping along the ocean floor.** To see what another nudibranch is up to, TURN TO PAGE 28.

CORAL POLYPS *(Cnidaria)*

The coral planula, or egg, settles on the rocky floor of the ocean. It has been drifting for weeks, but finally, it's found a perfect place to grow. It needs warm, shallow water where the waves aren't too rough. The planula starts to build a hard little skeleton around itself by soaking up minerals from the water. Inside this protective stone, the egg grows a **tentacle**. The egg becomes a coral polyp.

The polyp hunts. In the dark of the night, it stretches its flowery tentacle out of the hole of its shell. It snags plankton that drift by in the currents. Sometimes it even shoots out a line of sticky **mucus**. When something gets stuck in it, the polyp reels it in and snacks on its trapped **prey**.

Over time, the polyp links up with nearby polyps. Sometimes it even clones itself—it creates another identical polyp. These polyps unite and work so closely together that they share food and even their skeletons. As old ones die, new ones build on. Eventually, years and years later, these polyps will be big enough to form a mound of coral under the water. Some coral reefs in the ocean were started in this way more than 50 million years ago.

Last night for dinner, the coral polyp trapped . . .

Coral polyps feeding on plankton

Coral's Beauty Secret

The beautiful rainbow colors of the coral reef don't come from the coral. The color actually comes from the algae living inside the coral *(below, in lettuce coral)*. Soon after the coral turns into a polyp, it invites special algae into its cells. These algae aren't eaten by the coral. Instead, the algae live there peacefully, soaking up the sun during the day. This energy from the sun is turned into food that the coral uses.

...plankton. To see what other plankton are up to, TURN TO PAGE 18.

CORAL

If you're coming to this particular coral reef for shelter or a meal, you're out of luck. The coral stands white and ghostly in the water. Rising water temperatures from global warming caused the **algae** that live in coral to die off. Without the algae, the coral died. This is a **DEAD END**.

Even as you drift through the dying coral here, an anchor from a sightseeing boat extends into the water. It crunches through the dead staghorn coral and pierces the shell of a brain coral. This reef is already dying, but boaters, snorkelers, and fishers destroy living coral all the time. It may be hundreds of years before it can grow back again, if at all.

Unfortunately, warmer water and careless people aren't the only dangers to the coral. Pollution from dumped chemicals in the ocean also kills the coral. So does water runoff from cities. Runoff causes too many nutrients to enter the water. Algae grows rapidly and takes oxygen that ocean plants need. Diseases also affect the coral. And without the coral, the millions of species that depend on the reef are at risk. In fact, coral reefs are the most **endangered** habitats in the world.

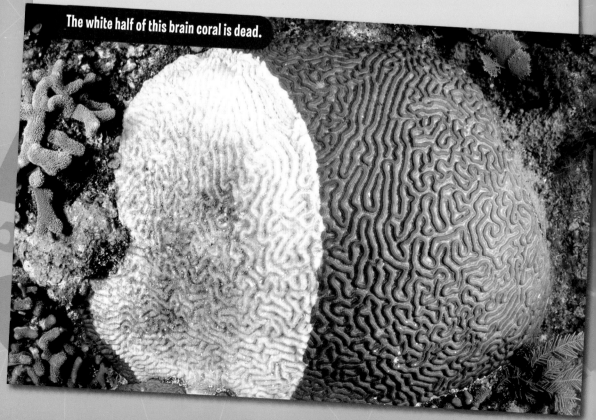

The white half of this brain coral is dead.

Attack of the Starfish

It's not just the coral reefs of the Caribbean that are in trouble. The reefs in the Indian and Pacific Oceans are threatened by a sudden increase in crown-of-thorns starfish. These starfish gobble coral at a rate of 2 square feet (0.2 square meters) a day. After they attack a reef, not much is left. Scientists aren't sure why there are suddenly so many more of these starfish. It might be natural for their numbers to increase and decrease in cycles. But it also might be that one of the crown-of-thorns' predators has disappeared.

SHARPNOSE PUFFER FISH *(Canthigaster rostrata)*

The puffer fish skirts along the edge of the staghorn coral. He stretches out his long snout to catch a clam between his teeth. He only has four teeth—two on top and two on the bottom—but they're perfect for pecking at hard coral, spiny urchins, and shellfish.

He flitters to shallow waters, taking a nibble here and there from the underwater jungle. Then, as he rounds a branch of a giant sea fan, he freezes. A barracuda! The long silver fish with the mouthful of teeth sees him at the same time. With a twitch of his tail, the barracuda zips toward the puffer.

But just as quickly, the puffer gulps water. As he sucks the water in, his body puffs out, just like a balloon being blown up. He doesn't have scales as most fish do. Instead, the tiny sharp spines that cover his body start to stick out. He becomes a round, prickly ball with a face. The barracuda coasts by, but the puffer fish looks too big and thorny to mess with. There must be something easier to eat. The barracuda swims on. Slowly, the puffer deflates. Whew! That was a close one.

Last night for dinner, the puffer fish pecked . . .

. . . coral polyps. To see what a group of coral polyps is up to, TURN TO PAGE 44.

. . . a long-horn nudibranch sliding down a staghorn coral. To see what another nudibranch is up to, TURN TO PAGE 28.

. . . coral. To see what coral is up to, TURN TO PAGE 46.

. . . nibbles off a sponge. To see what another sponge is up to, TURN TO PAGE 36.

. . . an Antillean scallop starting to burrow into the sand. To see what another scallop is up to, TURN TO PAGE 16.

. . . a black sea urchin scooting toward a nudibranch. To see what another sea urchin is up to, TURN TO PAGE 50.

. . . a banded coral shrimp searching for a fish to clean. To see what another shrimp is up to, TURN TO PAGE 52.

. . . a fan worm soaking in the nutrients from the water. To see what another fan worm is up to, TURN TO PAGE 38.

BLACK SEA URCHIN *(Diadema antillarum)*

As the light fades from the reef, the black sea urchin begins her nightly prowl. No really—she *is* moving. She just moves so slowly that it's hard to even notice. Those black spines—as long as your forearm—aren't just rippling in the waves. Ever so slowly, they are propelling her toward her new hunting spot. But the urchin isn't just a ball of spikes. Those spines are attached to a hard shell called a test. The test is the urchin's outer skeleton. It protects her inner parts.

Hours later, she joins the rest of the colony and settles on a crevice in the coral. Then she begins munching away on the **algae**. It may be hard to see the sea urchin move, but it's nearly impossible to see her eat. Her mouth is at the bottom of her body. Behind her mouth is a chewing organ called an Aristotle's lantern. It's an opening ringed by sharp teeth and bones that gnaw and grind at the coral to get at the algae, sponges, and any other creatures the urchin happens to find.

Last night for dinner, the urchin ground up . . .

An Important Link in the Food Chain

The black sea urchin is considered a keystone species of the reefs. That means that black sea urchins are so important to the coral reef that the habitat could not survive without them. In 1983 black sea urchins in the Caribbean began dying of a mystery disease. People were greatly concerned for the future of the Caribbean reefs. The disease traveled with the tides, and in the end, 97 percent of black sea urchins died. Decades later, the reefs are still struggling to recover.

. . . **plankton as it floats by.** To see what other plankton are up to, **TURN TO PAGE 18.**

. . . **a long-horn nudibranch.** To see what another nudibranch is up to, **TURN TO PAGE 28.**

. . . **a banded coral shrimp, injured by a barracuda.** To see what another shrimp is up to, **TURN TO PAGE 52.**

. . . **some coral polyps.** To see what a group of coral polpys is like, **TURN TO PAGE 44.**

. . . **a foureye butterflyfish that got too close.** To see what another butterflyfish is up to, **TURN TO PAGE 12.**

. . . **coral it was clinging to.** To see what a group of coral is like, **TURN TO PAGE 46.**

. . . **a fan worm.** To see what another fan worm is up to, **TURN TO PAGE 38.**

. . . **bits off a sponge.** To see what another sponge is up to, **TURN TO PAGE 36.**

BANDED CORAL SHRIMP *(Stenopus hispidus)*

The banded coral shrimp crawls out of the giant Caribbean sea anemone where it lives among the poisonous **tentacles**. She tiptoes up and over the coral to a top ledge. Once there, she starts waving her long **antennas**. Two of her neighbors scurry up to join her. Swaying back and forth, they dance. They are trying to attract customers.

Their tricks get noticed. A grouper pulls up in front of the shrimp. He stretches his fat-lipped mouth wide. His gills flare. But the shrimp doesn't run off. Instead, she steps right into the grouper's huge mouth and goes to work.

She pokes and prods, nibbling and munching. The grouper is covered in tiny **parasites** and worms—delicious! If the grouper and the shrimp crossed paths anywhere else but the cleaning station, the shrimp would be his dinner. But here she's safe.

Next in line is a parrot fish. But just as she climbs aboard, a blue green blur darts out and clamps down on her front claw. A trumpetfish attack!

The force of the attack knocks the shrimp off the parrot fish. She spins to the ocean floor. When she lands, she is missing her left front leg. Up above, the trumpetfish crunches on it.

The shrimp scrambles back to her anemone on nine legs. She'll be okay. The trumpetfish didn't tear off her leg. Her body just let it go. Doing this is a way to make a safe getaway and not get eaten entirely. In time, a new leg and claw will grow back. The new left leg will be smaller than the right, but it'll do the job.

Last night for dinner, the banded coral shrimp picked up . . .

. . . **bits and pieces of plankton.** To see what other plankton are up to, TURN TO PAGE 18.

. . . **black sea urchin eggs.** To see what another sea urchin is up to, TURN TO PAGE 50.

. . . **infected tissue from a hawksbill turtle.** To see what another hawksbill is up to, TURN TO PAGE 58.

. . . **mites from her anemone home.** To see what another giant Caribbean sea anemone is up to, TURN TO PAGE 54.

GIANT CARIBBEAN SEA ANEMONE

(Condylactis gigantea)

As the tide comes back in, the giant Caribbean sea anemone's **tentacles** unfold. The anemone may look like a plant growing out of the rocky bottom of the shore, but it's an animal. It clings to the rocks with a sticky leg called a pedal disk.

As the water comes in, the anemone creeps along the stone so slowly you can hardly see it move. That doesn't mean it doesn't care where it goes. As the anemone bumps against its neighbors, it pushes hard to move the other anemone out of the way. Soon a slow-motion fight breaks out as the two anemones battle for the best position on the rock. They push and shove and don't hesitate to lash out at each other with their poisonous tentacles.

Hours pass and the tide comes up farther. The anemone and its neighbors are well underwater. They turn their attention to hunting instead of fighting. A young squirrelfish swims by. The anemone can't go after it. But when the next

The giant Caribbean sea anemone's tentacles are dangerous to many reef creatures. But anemones and other creatures often team up. Anemones sometimes give crabs or fish a hiding place. In return, the anemones feed on the scraps of food the crab or fish leaves behind. Anemones use other fish as bait. The fish hang out by the anemone and draw in bigger predator fish. The anemone eats the predator fish. The anemone gets a meal, and the smaller fish have one less predator to worry about. When a creature helps another in this way, it is called symbiosis. The most famous team is the clownfish and the anemone. The clownfish lives inside the tentacles of the anemone, protected from the tentacles' poison by a special mucus layer.

wave washes the squirrelfish close to the anemone, it attacks. As soon as the fish brushes the anemone, the anemone shoots out its tentacles. The tentacles have tiny stingers called barbs. Each barb shoots poison into the squirrelfish. The poison stuns the fish. Then the tentacles guide the fish to the center of the anemone, where an open mouth is waiting. Mmm. Dinner.

Last night for dinner, the anemone digested . . .

. . . **a foureye butterflyfish that swam too close.** To see what another butterflyfish is up to, TURN TO PAGE 12.

. . . **a queen parrot fish that brushed up against the anemone.** To see what another queen parrot fish is up to, TURN TO PAGE 34.

. . . **a trumpetfish that got caught in the low tide.** To see what another trumpetfish is up to, TURN TO PAGE 20.

. . . **a long-horn nudibranch caught at the end of a slow-motion chase.** To see what another nudibranch is up to, TURN TO PAGE 28.

. . . **a remora that drifted into the anemone's tentacles.** To see what another remora is up to, TURN TO PAGE 14.

. . . **a baby smalltooth sawfish.** To see what another smalltooth sawfish is up to, TURN TO PAGE 33.

. . . **a banded coral shrimp that washed across the anemone.** To see what another shrimp is up to, TURN TO PAGE 52.

CARIBBEAN MONK SEAL *(Monachus tropicalis)*

Sorry, the Caribbean monk seal is a *DEAD END*. These seals used to cruise through the shallow waters of the reefs. They pulled themselves onto the beach to sun themselves and have their young. But as more tourists flocked to the beaches and to the water, the seals began disappearing. Monk seals dislike being around people. They will even leave their babies behind to die if they feel crowded by humans. People also hunted the monk seal for their meat, fur, and fat. While not officially **extinct**, the last time anyone saw one was in 1952.

Their close relatives, the Hawaiian monk seals and the Mediterranean monk seals, may be next. The Hawaiian monk seal is the most **endangered marine** animal in the United States. The Mediterranean monk seal is on the critically endangered list. That means if something is not done to help them, they too will become extinct.

An illustration of a Caribbean monk seal

Deep Divers

Technically, monk seals are land animals with four flippers and lots of fat, called blubber, to keep them warm and afloat. But monk seals are more comfortable in the water than onshore. They dive as deep as 2,000 feet (610 meters) for their meals. When they dive, their body sends their blood only to their brain and not their other organs. This makes the oxygen in their blood last as long as possible. They can even sleep in the water! They just hold their

THE HAWKSBILL TURTLE *(Eretmochelys imbricata)*

The hawksbill turtle—the size of a garbage can lid—glides through a school of butterflyfish. Just a swish of her flippers turns her body in the water. She slows as she swims past a branch of coral, and she takes a bite. Ouch! It's stinging coral—her face will soon be peeling where it touched the coral. But it was worth it to her. She's trying to get extra calcium for the eggs she'll lay soon.

She lets the incoming tide push her closer to shore. When her feet hit the sand, she starts pushing herself forward up the beach. Out of the water, her body seems impossibly heavy. Slowly, she scoots toward a little spot near a piece of driftwood. She digs. Then she turns and lays her first clutch of eggs. What look like 130 table tennis balls glisten in the moonlight. Then she carefully tucks them in with a blanket of sand.

Her job done, the turtle heaves herself back to the ocean. Bright eyes from the trees nearby watch her leave. Then, with a flurry of sand, the waiting mongoose finds the turtle's hidden treasure. He sucks down as many eggs as he can eat. The rest he leaves uncovered. Without the protective warmth of the sand, the remaining eggs won't survive.

Dozens of turtles once laid their eggs on this beach at night. With that many nests, one mongoose raid didn't do much harm to the turtle population. But tonight this hawksbill's nest was the only one on the beach. And that is the case all around the world for hawksbill turtles. They are critically **endangered** because of fishing and nest destruction. People have hunted the turtles for their beautiful shells. And that's why this is a *DEAD END*.

Not Enough Turtles

Already the reef has noticed the loss of the hawksbill turtles. The turtles eat mostly sponges—almost 1,200 pounds (544 kilograms) a year! Sponges have important roles in the coral reef. But without hawksbill turtles as their predators, the sponges have taken over the reef in some places. The coral itself is a living creature. When there are too many sponges, they block the coral from getting sunlight. And without sunlight, the coral can't survive.

GLOSSARY

algae: a plant or plantlike living thing

antenna: a long, thin feeler on an animal's head

carbon dioxide: a gas that animals give off and plants breathe in

carnivore: an animal that eats other animals

decomposers: living things, such as insects or bacteria, that feed on dead plants and animals

electrosense: a sensitivity to the weak electrical currents that fish give off

endangered: in danger of dying out

extinct: no longer existing, all kinds have died out

food chain: a system in which energy moves from the sun to plants and to animals as each eats and is eaten

food web: many food chains linked together. Food webs show how plants, animals, and other living things are connected in a habitat.

habitat: an area where a particular group of plants or animals naturally lives and grows

keystone species: a species that affects a large number of other animals

larva: the wormlike stage in some animals' lives between the egg and the adult forms

marine: of or from the ocean

mucus: a slimy material produced by the body

nutrients: substances, especially in food, that help a plant or animal survive

oxygen: a gas that animals and plants need to survive

parasite: an animal that lives on another animal and gets its food from it

phytoplankton: tiny bits of algae that float in the ocean currents

predators: animals that hunt and kill other animals for food

prey: animals that are hunted for food by other animals

primary consumers: animals that eat plants

producers: living things, such as plants, that make their own food

secondary consumers: animals and insects that eat other animals and insects

tentacle: a long, flexible body part used for movement or for capturing food

tertiary consumers: animals that eat other animals and that have few natural enemies

zooplankton: tiny animals that float in the ocean and can't move on their own

FURTHER READING AND WEBSITES

Burns, Loree Griffin. *Tracking Trash: Flotsam, Jetsam, and the Science of Ocean Motion*. New York: Houghton Mifflin, 2007. Find out why we need to protect our oceans from pollution in this highly acclaimed book.

Cerullo, Mary M. *Coral Reef: A City That Never Sleeps*. New York: Dutton, 1996. Dive into the photographs in this book for the next best thing to visiting a coral reef.

Cerullo, Mary M., and Beth E. Simmons. *Sea Secrets: Tiny Clues to a Big Mystery*. Lafayette, CO: Moonlight Publishing, 2009. This book explores problems with three ocean animals and links their trouble to a break in the food chain.

Collard, Sneed B., III. *One Night in the Coral Sea*. Watertown, MA: Charlesbridge, 2005. Take a tour through the Great Barrier Reef in Australia.

Enchanted Learning
http://www.enchantedlearning.com/biomes/coralreef/coralreef.shtml
Read about the animals of the coral reef and then print out coloring pages of them.

Gibbon, Gail. *Coral Reefs*. New York: Holiday House, 2007. Gibbon's simple text and pictures explore the coral reef habitat.

Kids Do Ecology
http://www.nceas.ucsb.edu/nceas-web/kids/biomes/coralreef.html
This site provides information on corals, as well as puzzles and games about the habitat.

Macaulay, Kelley, and Bobbie Kalman. *Coral Reef Food Chains*. New York: Crabtree, 2005. Learn more about what eats what in the coral reef habitat.

Walker, Sally M. *Reefs*. Minneapolis: Lerner Publications Company, 2008. This book introduces different kinds of reefs and explains why they are in danger around the world.

SELECTED BIBLIOGRAPHY

Center for Biological Diversity. "Caribbean Coral." *Center for Biological Diversity*. March 14, 2007. http://www.biologicaldiversity.org/swcbd/SPECIES/coral/ (November 17, 2008).

Dance, S. Peter. *Shells*. New York: Dorling Kindersley, 2002.

Lampton, Christopher. *Coral Reefs in Danger*. Brookfield, CT: Millbrook Press, 1992.

Lieske, Ewald, and Robert Myers. *Coral Reef Fishes: Caribbean, Indian Ocean, and Pacific Ocean Including the Red Sea*. Princeton, NJ: Princeton University Press, 1996.

MarineBio Society. *MarineBio.org*. N.d. http://www.marinebio.org/ (November 17, 2008).

McGavin, George C. *Endangered Wildlife on Brink of Extinction*. Buffalo: Firefly, 2006.

Pitkin, Linda. *Coral Fish*. Washington, DC: Smithsonian Institution Press, 2001.

Reef Education Network. "Problems and Solutions." *Reef Education Network*. N.d. http://www.reef.edu.au/ps.html (November 17, 2008).

———. "Who's Who?" *Reef Education Network*. N.d. http://www.reef.edu.au/contents/fr_who.html (17 November, 2008).

Reef Relief. "Coral Reef Ecosystem."*Reef Relief*. N.d. http://www.reefrelief.org/reef.shtml (November 17, 2008).

Sammon, Rick. *Rhythm of the Reef: A Day in the Life of the Coral Reef*. Stillwater, MN: Voyageur Press, 1995.

Sheppard, Charles. *Coral Reefs: Ecology, Threats, and Conservation*. Stillwater, MN: Voyageur Press, 2002.

Smith, C. Lavett. *National Audubon Society Field Guide to Tropical Marine Fishes: Caribbean, Gulf of Mexico, Florida, Bahamas, Bermuda*. New York: Knopf, 1997.

Wilson, Roberta, and James Q. Wilson. *Watching Fishes: Life and Behavior on Coral Reefs*. New York: Harper and Row, 1985.

INDEX

algae, 18, 29, 30, 34–35, 37, 38–39, 45–46, 50

Antillean scallop *(Bractechlamys antillarum)*, 14, 16–17, 21, 27, 41, 43, 49

banded coral shrimp *(Stenopus hispidus)*, 21, 27, 36, 41, 43, 49, 51, 52–53, 56

black sea urchin *(Diadema antillarum)*, 35, 41, 42–43, 48–49, 50–51, 53

Caribbean, 4, 33, 50

Caribbean monk seal *(Monachus tropicalis)*, 11, 19, 23, 31, 39, 57

cleaning station, 20, 24, 52

consumer, definition of, 6

coral *(Cnidaria)*, 44–47; as food, 12–13, 29, 34–35, 49, 51, 58; types, 4

coral reef, health of, 6, 30, 33, 46–47, 50, 59

fan worm *(Sabellida)*, 13, 29, 35, 38–39, 49, 51

food web, 6, 18, 22, 50; diagram of, 32

foureye butterflyfish *(Chaetodon capistratus)*, 12–13, 15, 21, 31, 51, 56, 58

giant Caribbean sea anemone *(Condylactis gigantea)*, 12–13, 19, 29, 43, 52–53, 54–56

great barracuda *(Sphyraena barracuda)*, 7, 11, 15, 19, 22–23, 31, 48

hawksbill turtle *(Eretmochelys imbricata)*, 11, 19, 31, 36, 39, 53, 58–59

humans, 36; and animal attacks, 9, 22; and evidence in coral reef, 10, 22, 46; as fishers and hunters, 14, 17, 33, 46, 57, 59; and seafood, 22; as

scientists, 47; as tourists, 57

keystone species, 50

long-horn nudibranch *(Austraeolis catina)*, 27, 28–29, 41, 43, 49, 51, 56

map, 5

photosynthesis (diagram), 30

plankton, 13, 16–17, 18–19, 29, 35, 36–37, 44–45, 51, 53

plants, 6, 18, 20, 30–31, 33, 38

poison, 22, 26, 28, 52, 54–55

queen parrotfish *(Scarus vetula)*, 11, 15, 20–21, 34–35, 39, 52, 56

queen triggerfish *(Balistes vetula)*, 11, 15, 21, 23, 39, 42–43

remora *(Echeneis naucrates)*, 14–15, 19, 21, 23, 56

sea grass, 30

sea slug. *See* long-horn nudibranch

shark sucker. *See* remora

sharpnose puffer fish *(Canthigaster rostrata)*, 11, 15, 21, 23, 48–49

smalltooth sawfish *(Pristis pectinata)*, 7, 23, 31, 33, 56

southern stingray *(Dasyatis americana)*, 11, 15, 16, 23, 24–27, 31, 39

sponges *(Porifera)*, 5, 36–37, 59; as food, 12–13, 19, 29, 34–35, 39, 49, 50–51, 59

spotted moray eel *(Gymnothorax moringa)*, 7, 15, 19, 23, 27, 40–41

tiger shark *(Galeocerdo cuvier)*, 6, 7, 8–11, 19, 31, 39

trumpetfish *(Aulostomus maculatus)*, 11, 20–21, 23, 31, 52, 56

Photo Acknowledgments

The images in this book are used with the permission of: © Mike Kelly/The Image Bank/Getty Images, pp. 1, 4–5, 6–7, 11, 13, 15, 17, 19, 21, 23, 27, 29, 31, 35, 37, 39, 41, 43, 45, 49, 51, 53, 56; © Bill Hauser/Independent Picture Service (map), p. 5; © Biosphoto/ Brandon Cole/Peter Arnold, Inc., p. 8; © Brian J. Skerry/National Geographic/Getty Images, p. 9; © Biosphoto/Peter Arnold, Inc., p. 10; © Larry Lipsky/DRK PHOTO, p. 12; © Jeff Rotman/Iconica/ Getty Images, p. 14; © Femorale, Ltd., p. 16; © Jim Simmen/Photographer's Choice/Getty Images, p. 18; © www.Norbert Wu.com, p. 20 (top); © Reinhard Dirscherl/SeaPics.com, p. 20 (bottom); © Mark Conlin/SeaPics.com, p. 22; © Espen Rekdal/SeaPics.com, pp. 24, 54; © Doug Perrine/SeaPics.com, pp. 25, 33, 36 (top), 50; © Jeff Rotman/SeaPics.com, p. 26; © Kasey Canton/ Deepseaimages.com, p. 28; © Brandon Cole/Visuals Unlimited/Getty Images, pp. 30, 36 (bottom), 46; © David Doubilet/National Geographic/Getty Images, p. 34; © Federico Cabello/SuperStock, p. 38; © George Grall/National Geographic/Getty Images, p. 40; © Stuart Westmorland/Danita Delimont.com, p. 42; © Scott Leslie/Minden Pictures, p. 44; © M.C. Chamberlain/DRK PHOTO, p. 45 (top); © Kike Calvo/Visual & Written SL/Alamy, p. 47; Robert A. Patzner, p. 48; © Brandon Cole/Visuals Unlimited, Inc., p. 52; © Doug Perrine/ naturepl.com, p. 55; © Richard Ellis/SeaPics.com, p. 57; © Reinhard Dirscherl/ Visuals Unlimited, Inc., p. 58; © Morales Morales/age fotostock/Photolibrary, p. 59. Illustrations for game board and pieces © Bill Hauser/Independent Picture Service.

Front cover: (main) © Mike Kelly/The Image Bank/Getty Images, (thumbnails) © Brian J. Skerry /National Geographic/Getty Images (left); © Jeff Hunter/ Photographer's Choice/Getty Images (second from left); © Brandon Cole Marine Photography /Alamy, (second from right)© Sue Flood/The Image Bank/Getty Images (right).

About the Authors

Don Wojahn and Becky Wojahn are school library media specialists by day and writers by night. Their natural habitat is the temperate forests of northwestern Wisconsin, where they share their den with two animal-loving sons and two big black dogs. The Wojahns are the authors of all twelve books in the Follow that Food Chain series.